2.95

W9-AKE-795

Collect, Print and Paint from Nature

In this world we live in we are surrounded by
the grace and beauty of nature. The leaves, flowers,
moss and ferns in a beech-maple forest, for example,
all have their individual patterns which mold together
to make a larger design in nature.

By bringing home leaves and other specimens from
the woods and fields and by making prints or paintings
with them, you become more aware of their shape and
beauty. And by placing them in different designs
as you paint, you create your personal impression
of the trip you took.

Collect, Print and Paint from Nature

by John Hawkinson

ALBERT WHITMAN & COMPANY · CHICAGO

PRINTING

For the printing of leaves you need the simplest of equipment—a brush, a jar of water, some water colors, library paste, newspapers and construction paper. Leaves should be pressed in a book for a week before printing. In fact, you can keep them for as long as a year before using. If they become too brittle, soak them in water.

Leaves

Put a small amount of paste on a dish.

Put a little water on the colors you plan to use.

Cut newspaper into sheets about 6 by 8 inches in size. Place a leaf on one of the pieces of newspaper.

Dip your brush in the water, then draw the brush along the top of the jar to remove some of the water. Now put the brush on the paste and gently rub it back and forth until some of the paste becomes liquid and sticks to the brush.

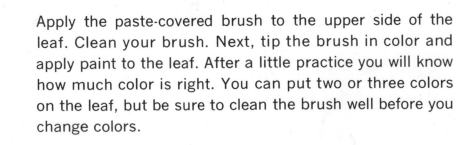

Apply the paste-covered brush to the upper side of the leaf. Clean your brush. Next, tip the brush in color and apply paint to the leaf. After a little practice you will know how much color is right. You can put two or three colors on the leaf, but be sure to clean the brush well before you change colors.

4

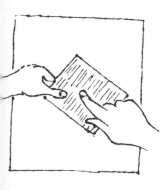

Place the leaf on construction paper, painted side down. Put a clean sheet of newspaper over the leaf. Hold the leaf in place by the stem and rub over the leaf gently with your thumb or one finger. Lift up the leaf by its stem and see what has happened.

Tempera colors may be used, but you will not need paste. Clean and use the brush just as carefully as with water colors.

Cattails, Moss and Stones

Many things besides leaves that you find outdoors can be used for printing. One of the most interesting of these is the cattail.

Cut the stem of a cattail about six inches from the tail and let the cattail soak in a jar of water for a few minutes.

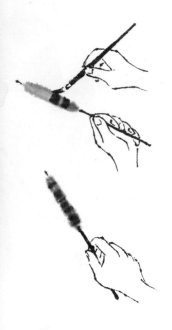

Then with a brush apply color to the cattail in stripes, twisting the cattail with your other hand. Put on as many colors as you like. (Be sure to clean your brush each time that you put on a new color.)

Now the fun begins. By holding the cattail by the stem you can pat it down, roll it, or rub it across the paper. Try several sheets of paper, just experimenting.

Moss is very easy to print with. Take a small piece dipped in moist color and pat it on your paper.

To make stone prints, first find smooth, flat stones from a beach. Apply color with a brush to one side of the stone and then press the stone firmly on paper.

SPATTER PRINTING

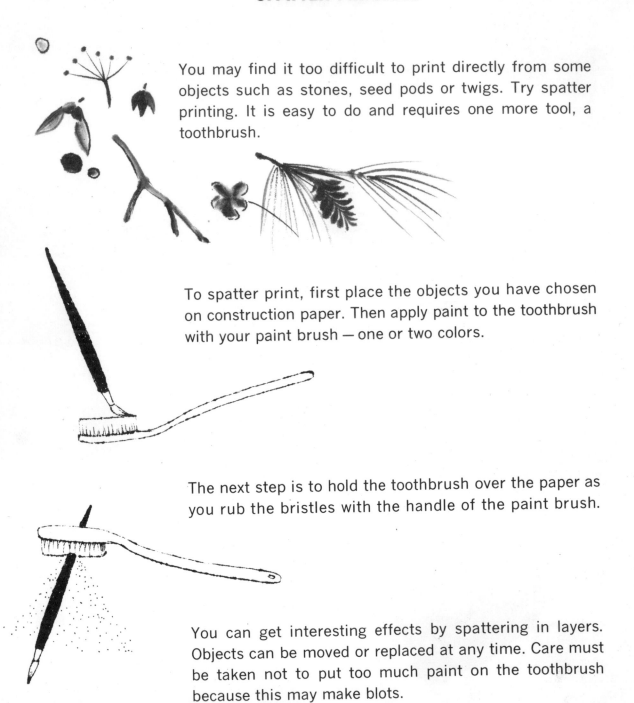

You may find it too difficult to print directly from some objects such as stones, seed pods or twigs. Try spatter printing. It is easy to do and requires one more tool, a toothbrush.

To spatter print, first place the objects you have chosen on construction paper. Then apply paint to the toothbrush with your paint brush — one or two colors.

The next step is to hold the toothbrush over the paper as you rub the bristles with the handle of the paint brush.

You can get interesting effects by spattering in layers. Objects can be moved or replaced at any time. Care must be taken not to put too much paint on the toothbrush because this may make blots.

PAINTING

The equipment for painting is the same as that for printing: a jar of water, a brush (about size 10 or 12), and water colors or tempera — water colors preferred.

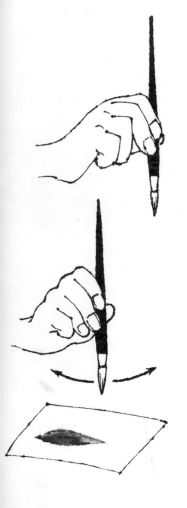

Leaves

The brush is a tool that must be held correctly and moved gracefully or it will produce nothing. Hold it at the balance with your thumb and two fingers, as shown. The balance is the thickest part of the brush handle.

The wrist and arm are straight and parallel to the paper. Now move the brush from side to side like a pendulum by moving only the wrist. This wrist stroke will make it easy for you to paint narrow leaves like the willow leaf.

Let's try. Place a willow leaf in front of you for a model. Construction paper or newsprint will do for your painting.

Moisten each pan of water color with a few drops of water from the brush.

10

Now dip the brush in the water and draw the brush across the top of the jar to remove some of the water.

Dip the brush in yellow until it becomes well filled with color, then put just the tip of the brush in blue or green.

Place the tip of the brush on the paper and slowly rotate your wrist. If you are holding your brush correctly, the point should follow the center of the leaf and leave the paper at the end of the leaf.

1   2

You can make the leaves point in any direction if you twist your body or move your elbow, but always keep your wrist and forearm parallel to the paper.

Some leaves are too broad to make with one stroke of the brush. Take an ash leaf and place it on a piece of paper.

Draw the outline of the leaf. Add the center vein to guide your stroke for the first few times.

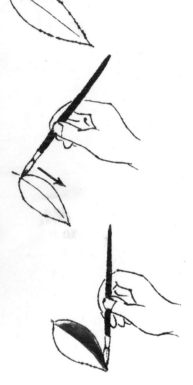

Clean your brush and add color just as you did for the willow leaf. Now, put the tip of the brush on the center line at the stem, holding the brush as shown.

Follow the center line with the tip of the brush. Where the leaf becomes wider, press the base of the brush down, then up again, to form the end of the leaf. If you are right-handed, this will be the right half of the leaf.

The easiest way to do the other half of the leaf is to turn the paper completely around. You will be able to do the other part with the same stroke, in reverse. This is a finger stroke with the heel of your hand resting on the paper.

12

Many trees, like maples and the oaks, have beautiful but more complex leaves than those of the ash and the willow. The sugar maple, which turns such beautiful colors in the fall, is a good example to begin with. It is almost as easy to paint as the ash or elm. Draw around the leaf, and, after removing the leaf, put in the principal veins, as shown.

Use the brush in the same way as in painting an ash leaf, following each vein to the end on one side of a section, then turning the paper around to do the other side.

Try other kinds of leaves like the maple and see if you can work out the right stroke for each one. After you have the rhythm of the stroke, you can eliminate the outlines and work with the leaf in front of you.

14

Tree Trunks, Stems

Every kind of tree has its own kind of trunk. Some are smooth, some are rough. Most of them are straight and strong.

To paint a tree trunk, hold the brush with thumb and two fingers. Wrist and forearm are parallel to the paper, elbow out to the side.

After applying colors, place the brush tip at the bottom of the paper and draw it up to the top of the paper with the same action you use in rolling a ball. Use your arm and elbow only.

If just the brush tip touches the paper, the line will be thin. Press the brush all the way down and the line will become broad.

A wet brush makes a smooth trunk. A dry brush makes a rough trunk.

Long leaves of cattails and tulips can also be done with this arm stroke. Start with the tip of the brush on the paper. As you draw the brush up toward the top of the paper, bear down and then up again to form the leaf.

Every branch of every tree or bush reaches for the sun. The leaves grow from the branches in the spring, and new branches form. In the winter, the tree and its branches stop growing and rest.

Find a branch or twig. An old dead one lying on the ground will do. It should have branches but no leaves. Put it in a vase or something to hold it and place it in front of you. Notice that wherever there is a joint, there is a little bulge or lump. Notice also that the twig may appear to curve, but if you look closely you will see a series of short or long joints with slight bulges wherever the direction changes.

To paint, apply color to your brush. Hold the brush as you did for the arm stroke. Put the tip of your brush on the paper and make the twig grow with your brush. Hesitate a little for every joint or change of direction. It is important to keep looking at the twig when painting. In fact, you will find it possible to paint without looking at the paper at all. The little twigs near the top of the branch can be done with the finger stroke or the wrist stroke.

Flowers

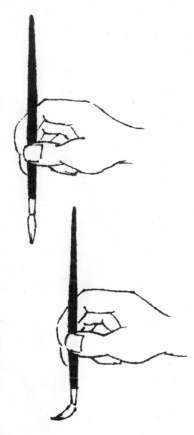

Many things from nature — flowers, nuts, small leaves, buds, pussy willows — can be painted with a press stroke. The brush is merely pressed down on the paper after one, two, or even three colors have been added.

The brush is held as for the wrist or arm stroke, arm and wrist horizontal to the paper and the brush vertical to the paper.

The brush point touches the paper first. By slightly slanting the brush you can direct the press stroke.

When painting flowers, try to have them in front of you as models. If this is not possible, photographs will do.

Flowers can be painted from the center or from the end of each petal. The coloring of the flower will determine this. Stems and leaves can be done with wrist and arm strokes.

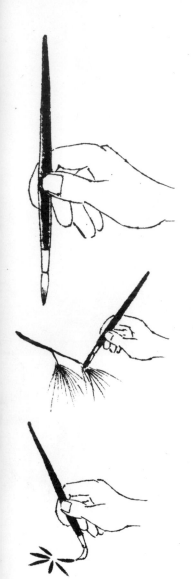

You have by now, I hope, mastered the wrist and arm strokes, so be brave and try the most difficult stroke. This is the finger stroke. As a matter of fact, you have probably already tried one kind of finger stroke, described on page 12.

The brush is held as shown in the picture. Notice that the thumb and forefinger are together and the index finger is below and a little behind the brush. In this stroke, only the fingers move. The arm and wrist remain stationary and parallel to the paper.

Try painting pine needles first. This is easy because the brush moves in the same direction each time.

Now try the aster or daisy type of flower. This is difficult at first, and you must concentrate on not moving anything but your fingers. This doesn't mean that you can't move the paper.

Last, try the tulip, which is done with a twist of the wrist and a flick of the fingers, as shown. Then, with the arm stroke, add the stem and the leaves.

22

THE CITY

At first glance, the city doesn't seem to have much to offer an artist who is interested in nature. And if a child is looking for adventure, he may not find the city as exciting as going to a river or to a beach.

But if you can ignore the buildings and the people of the city and look for the growing things you may find that you are living at a crossroad of the plant world.

In a city, the Japanese maple, the European birch and Dutch tulip may grow in the same yard with the American elm and Kentucky bluegrass. The variety and beauty of these growing things are always there for us to see. It just takes a little hunting. Going down the streets and up the alleys, making a leaf collection is in itself an adventure. There is always the next street that may have new specimens for you.

24

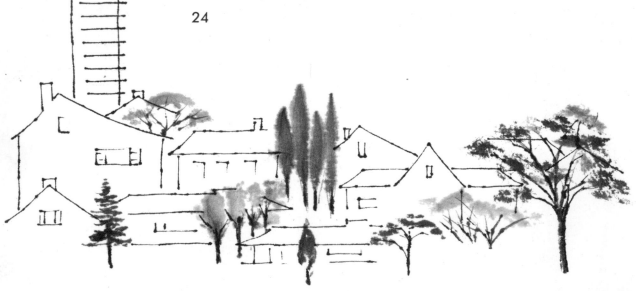

THE WAYSIDE

The next time that you are traveling on a country road — a quiet road through farmland — find a place to stop and look around for things that grow.

Wayside flowers, simple and small, grow everywhere, and no one minds if you pick a few. There are little asters, daisies, chickory, dandelions and goldenrod — always something to see from spring until late fall. Most of these flowers won't keep very well, so it is foolish to pick a large bouquet.

Take a few flowers and remember how they grow. Press them in a book and take them home to paint from.

Other things grow along the road — small bushes, sumac, grapevines, little trees — mostly weeds that nobody wants on farms or in yards. And these outcasts of the plant world form a lovely pattern of nature for all to see.

26

THE OAK FOREST

In America we have what is known as a black oak forest. In this forest there are other kinds of trees as well, white oak, sassafrass, black cherry, shadbush, witch hazel, dogwood and many more.

The black oak and white oak are tall and form the forest's ceiling. The other trees are content to dwell in their shade.

Oak trees are the last to leaf in the spring and the last to drop their leaves in autumn. Some of them even keep their leaves through the winter.

Oak forests are fairly open and hilly, and the underbrush is sometimes thick. There is enough sunshine coming through the trees so that grass will come up here and there, and blueberries grow on the ground.

The Indians who lived in the oak forests made bread from the acorns, dried the berries, and hunted the animals there. Oak forests today serve no such purpose, but their beauty is the same and is there for us to enjoy.

28

THE BEECH-MAPLE FOREST

Of the hardwood forests in this country, the beech-maple is the most like a storybook forest.

The beech and maple trees grow straight and tall, sometimes a hundred feet high. Beeches with smooth gray trunks and maples with their rough trunks form the columns, while their high branches come together to form arches that give the look and feel of a cathedral.

Smaller trees like ironwood and witch hazel are not so plentiful. The ground cover is usually sparse, and partridgeberry, wild geranium and other colorful plants grow here and there. There are no thickets to bar your way, and the woods seem to invite you to wander through them quietly.

30

THE BEACH

What is more wonderful on a hot day than to run on a sandy beach down to the water's edge! Feel the water with your hands. Take off your shoes and run back and forth like a sandpiper. Then look down at your feet and see all the smooth, round pebbles. How bright they are in the water. They are duller on the sand, but what a beautiful mosaic they make. Dark blue, light brown, red, green — together they make another design of nature.

The linden, the cedar and the cottonwood love to live near a beach. Sand cherry and grass that is sharp and tough grow with other plants near the beach. The sand shows tracks of toads, gulls, crows, and sometimes the huge tracks of the heron.

Other things such as seaweeds, shells, fossils, insects and driftwood tossed on the beach by the water, make more patterns to use for painting or printing. The sky, the gulls overhead, the waves and the bright, hot sand complete the impression of the beach.

32

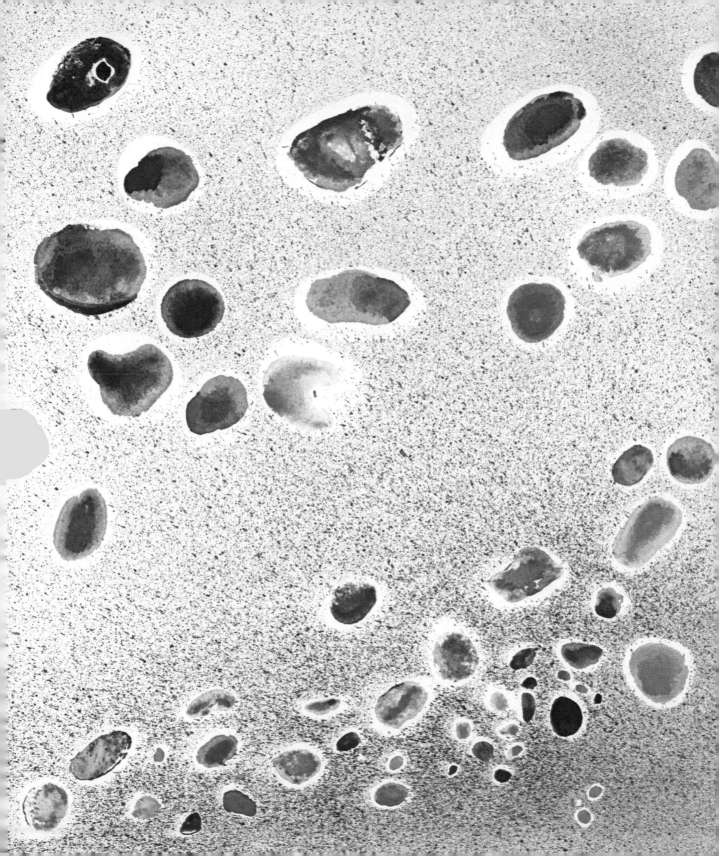

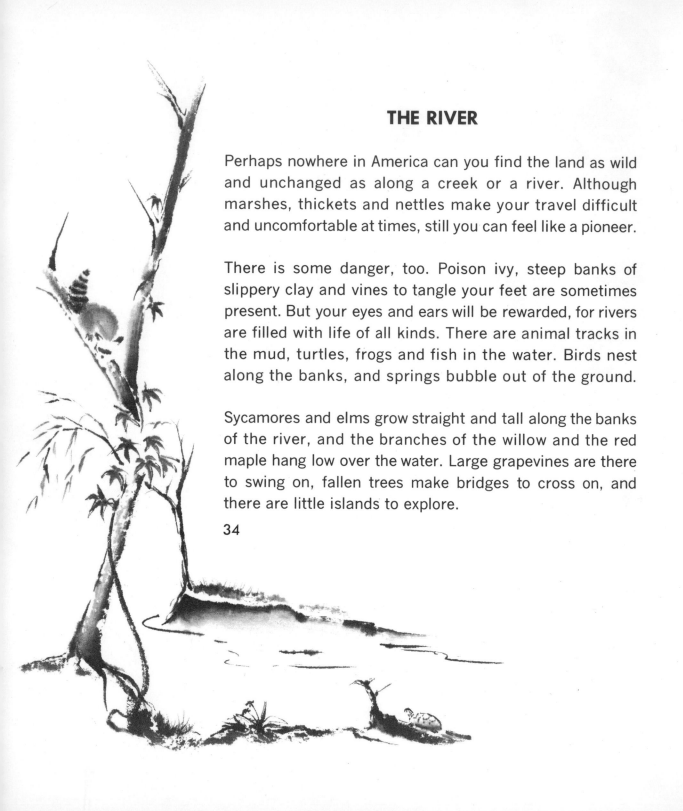

THE RIVER

Perhaps nowhere in America can you find the land as wild and unchanged as along a creek or a river. Although marshes, thickets and nettles make your travel difficult and uncomfortable at times, still you can feel like a pioneer.

There is some danger, too. Poison ivy, steep banks of slippery clay and vines to tangle your feet are sometimes present. But your eyes and ears will be rewarded, for rivers are filled with life of all kinds. There are animal tracks in the mud, turtles, frogs and fish in the water. Birds nest along the banks, and springs bubble out of the ground.

Sycamores and elms grow straight and tall along the banks of the river, and the branches of the willow and the red maple hang low over the water. Large grapevines are there to swing on, fallen trees make bridges to cross on, and there are little islands to explore.

34

THE SWAMP

A journey to a swamp is an adventure that has a feeling of mystery about it. Frogs you can't see sing from the cattails. Strong smells, dark water, reeds waving in the wind, old dead logs and bright green moss are all part of the swamp.

A splash of water, a rustle in the grass will let you know that something is near by even if you can't see it. Swamps are very much alive with birds, animals and strange little insects.

Aspen leaves dance in the slightest breeze. Odd mushrooms grow on crumbling stumps. Ferns bend in graceful arches. Moss is soft and cool to the touch. Vines climb tree trunks and sometimes cover branches to make bowers for hiding.

There are many kinds of swamps. Some with tamarack and sumac, some with sour gum and buttonball, others with aspen and cherry, oak or maple. They all have the same air of mystery.

36

THE MOUNTAINS

Far away from most of us in this country are the Rocky Mountains. It is easy to be awed by their snow-capped peaks, towering cliffs and tall evergreens.

To get a more intimate view of these mountains, you should find a little stream and climb along its banks as it comes tumbling down. The stream will race over rocks, around boulders, through the forest and down into the grassy valleys.

And at every stream you can see a soft, gray bird called the water ouzel. He will be your companion as you journey along the stream. He will show you dark forests of pine, spruce and fir, the aspens with their dancing leaves, and alpine valleys with mountain flowers. Rocks of all colors, evergreen cones of different shapes and sizes, and the variety of needles and leaves make collecting fun.

38

In every season of the year and everywhere you go, you can find something to collect for painting or printing. This book tells you of just a little bit of what can be done with your field-trip experiences. You will think of all kinds of new experiments as you discover new places and observe new designs in nature.